QUOTATIONS FROM

JIMMY

DE

SANA

JANUARY 1988

PRIMARY INFORMATION

"ART IS A LIE THAT MAKES
US REALIZE TRUTH."
—Pablo Picasso

"I BELIEVE BECAUSE IT
IS IMPOSSIBLE."
—St. Augustine

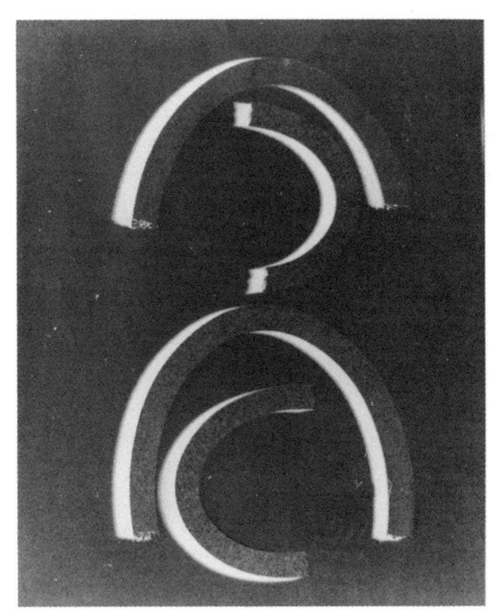

"BROKEN OVAL"

SOUL

A

PART OF

MY SOUL,

IS THE

SAME

AS

THE WHOLE.

PLAN

DESTROY

WHAT

YOU

DO NOT

MAKE,

AND

CREATE

WHAT

YOU

ATTEMPT TO

FAKE.

TRUTH

ALL

NIGHT

I WAITED

UNTIL

THE MADNESS

DROVE

THE

DESIRE

INTO

THE

MOMENT

THAT WE OFTEN

CALL TRUTH.

WHAT'S WORSE?

IF EVERYTHING

SEEMS

IMPOSSIBLE,

THEN

NOTHING

IS.

KNOWLEDGE

TO

TELL

THE TRUTH,

MY INNOCENCE,

ONCE ON LEAVE,

SINCE VANISHED,

NOW AND

THEN INVITED ME

TO

LIE.

CODE

VULGARITY

IS

ABSENT,

WHEN

SANCTITY

IS

PRESENT.

TIME

LIVING

ON

BORROWED TIME

IS

THE

SAME AS

LIVING.

AN EVENING OUT

SOON,

I WILL

PICK UP

THE NIGHT AIR

AND

SHY BACK

AND

FORTH

TILL

IT

STANDS UP

WITH ME.

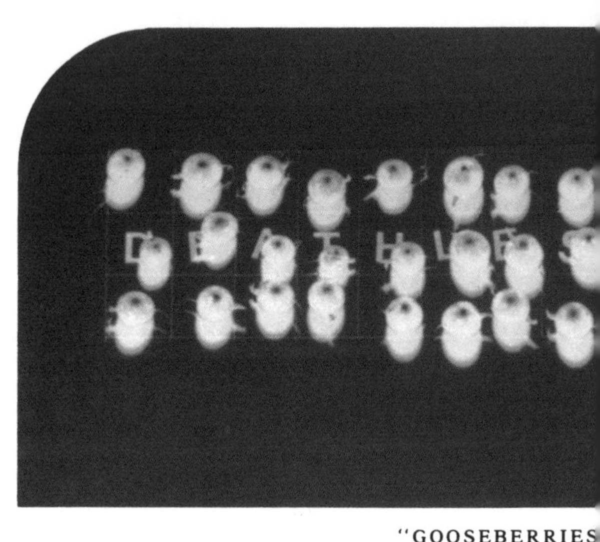

''GOOSEBERRIES

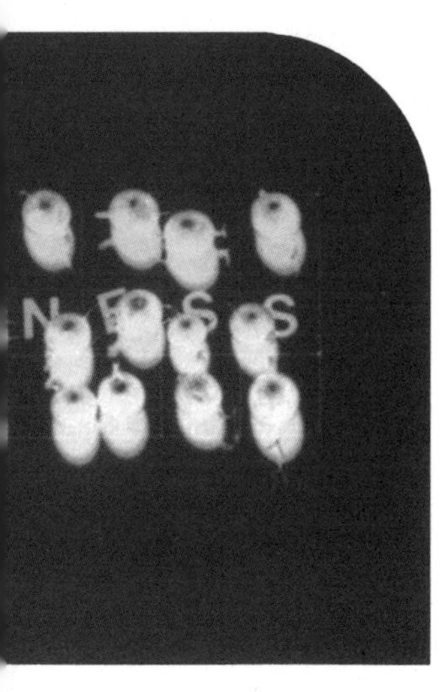

FOOL

HOW

LONG

CAN I

ACCEPT

THE FOOL

THAT I AM,

AS

NOT

A

FOOL

AT ALL.

THE COW

THE

COW

SAID

MOO, BUT

NOT

MY

COW

SAID

BOW WOW.

AN ANSWER

PROCLIVITY
MAKES
A PASSIVE
ADVANCE.

PROCLIVITY
UNDERMINES
RAPID
SEDUCTION.

PROCLIVITY
ADVANCES
INTO
RETREAT.

YOUR EARS

THE EXPRESSION
ON YOUR FACE,
PLUS YOUR
EARS,
MAKE ALL QUESTIONS
VANISH.

DESIRE

WHEN YOU
STEP
OVER THE
LINE,
THE
LINE BECOMES
YOU.

ART

WHEN
PATHOLOGY
BECOMES
A
METAPHOR,

ART
BECOMES
INDULGENCE.

INVENTION

ONE OF
THE TWO
THINGS
TO INVENT
IN THE FUTURE,
IS
A MACHINE
TO
STOP
THE OTHER.

HER OPTIMISM

SHE SAID
YOUR
EYES
LIGHT UP THE
MOON,
WHICH, TO THAT
I SAID,
SHE READS
WITH
NO EYES.

A SIMPLE SHOE

A
SIMPLE
SHOE
WOULD FIT
ON
ANY
FOOT
IF
THE
SIMPLE
SHOE
WAS ANY SIZE.

THE BEST

I
HAVE
DONE
(THE BEST)
IS
YET
TO COME.

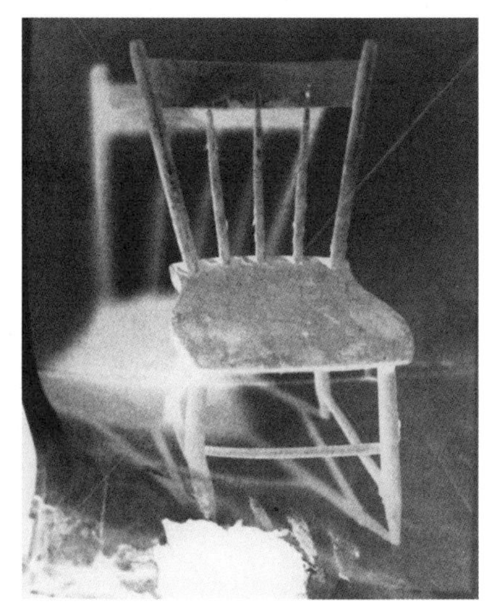

"CHAIR"

''DIE AT THE RIGHT TIME.''

—Nietzsche

979-8-9885736-5-4

Quotations from Jimmy DeSana was originally published in 1988 by Pat Hearn Gallery and was designed by Anthony McCall Associates. This is a facsimile edition published by Primary Information in 2024.